Dirty Jobs
Plumber

Simon Rose

www.av2books.com

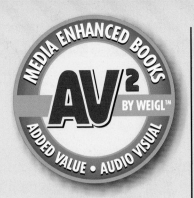

AV² provides enriched content that supplements and complements this book. Weigl's AV² books strive to create inspired learning and engage young minds in a total learning experience.

Your AV² Media Enhanced books come alive with...

Audio
Listen to sections of the book read aloud.

Key Words
Study vocabulary, and complete a matching word activity.

Video
Watch informative video clips.

Quizzes
Test your knowledge.

Embedded Weblinks
Gain additional information for research.

Slide Show
View images and captions, and prepare a presentation.

Try This!
Complete activities and hands-on experiments.

... and much, much more!

Go to **www.av2books.com**, and enter this book's unique code.

BOOK CODE

F325499

AV² by Weigl brings you media enhanced books that support active learning.

Published by AV² by Weigl
350 5ᵗʰ Avenue, 59ᵗʰ Floor
New York, NY 10118

Websites: www.av2books.com www.weigl.com

Library of Congress Cataloging-in-Publication Data

Rose, Simon, 1961-
  Plumber / Simon Rose.
    pages cm. -- (Dirty jobs)
Includes bibliographical references and index.
ISBN 978-1-4896-2994-4 (hard cover : alk. paper) -- ISBN 978-1-4896-2995-1 (soft cover : alk. paper) --
ISBN 978-1-4896-2996-8 (single user ebook) -- ISBN 978-1-4896-2997-5 (multi-user ebook)
1. Plumbing--Juvenile literature. 2. Plumbing--Vocational guidance--Juvenile literature. 3. Plumbers--Juvenile literature. I. Title.
TH6124.R67 2016
696'.1023--dc23
                              2014038987

Printed in the United States of America in Brainerd, Minnesota
1 2 3 4 5 6 7 8 9 0 19 18 17 16 15

012015
WEP051214

Senior Editor: Aaron Carr
Designer: Mandy Christiansen

Every reasonable effort has been made to trace ownership and to obtain permission to reprint copyright material. The publishers would be pleased to have any errors or omissions brought to their attention so that they may be corrected in subsequent printings.

Weigl acknowledges Getty Images as its primary image supplier for this title.

Contents

What Is a Plumber?

A plumber installs, repairs, and maintains pipes that are fitted in all types of buildings. These pipes are mostly used to carry drinking water. Plumbers also work on pipes and systems that are used for **drainage**, **irrigation**, and **sewage**. Plumbers work on both large and small projects. The word plumber comes from the **Latin** *plumbum*, which means "lead." Ancient Romans used lead to make pipes that carried water. Hundreds of years ago, anyone who worked with lead was called a plumber.

Pipefitters and steamfitters also work with pipes in buildings, but they deal with different kinds of materials than plumbers. Pipefitters work with pipes that carry chemicals and gases. They use materials such as steel and copper. Steamfitters work with pipes that move high-pressure fluids and gases. Pipefitters and steamfitters both install or repair controls for these systems.

There were **386,900** plumbers, pipefitters, and steamfitters in the U.S. in 2012.

More than **25 billion feet** (7.6 billion meters) of copper pipe has been laid in the U.S. since 1963. This could circle Earth 200 times.

Copper is the main metal used for plumbing today. It was also used for pipes in Ancient Egypt in 2500 BC.

Plumbers need to carefully measure each part of pipe. This is to make sure the pipes fit together and do not leak.

Where They Work

Plumbers work anywhere that pipes and water equipment are used. This includes houses and apartments. Plumbers install or fix **faucets**, drains, and pipes. They also work on kitchen and bathroom fixtures. These include sinks, dishwashers, toilets, showers, bathtubs, and water heaters.

Plumbers may work in homes, hospitals, schools, factories, offices, or government buildings. Many plumbers work while new homes are being built. They work on large and small construction jobs. These range from houses to high-rise buildings. Plumbers also make repairs on older homes. They install, maintain, and repair pipes, pumps, and other kinds of plumbing equipment.

Plumbers install pipes and other parts in hot water systems.

On Call

Plumbers are often called for emergencies. They might need to fix or replace pipes that have caused dangerous situations, such as floods. Sometimes, they are called out to public places where pipes may have burst. An emergency situation like this can cause many problems for the public. Plumbers often work on weekends, evenings, and holidays.

Plumbers can be called out to emergencies at any time of the day or night.

Plumbers carry most of their equipment in the back of their vans.

A Dirty Job

When a drain or pipe is blocked, plumbers have to remove whatever is stopping the flow of water. This is usually something very dirty. Hair, food, cooking fat, and grease can cause blocked drains. Paper that is washed down a drain can also get stuck in a pipe. Leaves and other garden material can block drains.

Sewage

Plumbers also unblock sewer pipes that run from toilets. Plumbers can be exposed to raw sewage. This is sewage that has not been treated to make it safe to handle. Raw sewage can cause diseases. Plumbers can also become ill from cleaning bird or rodent droppings from clogged pipes.

On construction sites, plumbers often work underground.

Plumbers also face dangers in the construction industry. These include cuts from sharp blades, injuries from power tools, and falls and burns. Plumbers might work with dangerous chemicals, such as lead, **sulfur dioxide**, and **asbestos**.

Over time, pipes may break down. They may rust, break, or develop holes. When this happens, the pipes usually need to be replaced.

Plumbers lay large pipes in the street to carry waste water from homes to sewers.

Plumbers face many hazards every day, no matter where they are working.

Plumbers can be in **danger** from **electric shocks.**

Most **plumbers** work alone. This means that they **may not receive help right away** if they are **injured.**

Plumbers can be **burned** by the sudden release of **hot water** or **steam** from pipes.

Plumbers can be exposed to mold. This can cause **breathing problems.**

All in a Day's Work

A plumber can do many jobs on a construction site. When a project starts, a plumber does layout work. This means they look at the building plans to decide where to put the plumbing. The plumber will work with other **tradespeople**. These include builders and electricians.

Plumbers can start work once they have all the materials they need. These materials include **cast iron**, copper, or plastic pipe. The type of material used depends on the type of project. The plumber checks for leaks or other problems while installing the pipes. Plumbing fixtures are added later. The plumber works with others at this stage. They check the plans to make sure that the correct model is installed in the proper place.

Sometimes, plumbers must work in small spaces.

A plumber's average work week is between **four and five days**.

When plumbers work outside normal working hours, they are usually paid at **1.5 times** their normal hourly rate.

Plumbers typically work from **8 to 10** hours per day.

Water Supply and Drainage

Piping systems transport water in and out of buildings. Some pipes bring clean water into a home. This is used for drinking, washing clothes, and for toilets. Water is also sent to water heaters and used for showers, bathtubs, and faucets. Other pipes move dirty water out of a home. This water is sent to drains and sewers.

heated water

water heater

clean water

dirty water

Staying Safe

Plumbers work with knives, saws, and other sharp objects. They also work with chemicals and **biohazards**. These can harm the skin or are poisonous. Plumbers use safety clothing and equipment to protect them from these dangers.

Safety Glasses

Plumbers use safety glasses to protect their eyes from flying pieces of wood or metal. This can happen when unblocking drains or when using saws or hammers. Plumbers may also lay down and look up to inspect a drain. While doing this, small objects might fall on them.

Facemask

If plumbers are using saws or **sanding**, facemasks keep them from breathing in dust. When plumbers work with sewage pipes, they might breathe in hydrogen sulphide. This is a poisonous gas in sewers. It smells like rotten eggs. This gas can cause serious health issues. Facemasks protect the plumber.

Safety First

Plumbers must wear safety equipment. Many companies provide equipment and uniforms for their workers. Others ask plumbers to buy their own gear.

Hardhat

Plumbers wear hardhats when working on construction sites. This protects them from things that can fall on them. It also protects the plumber's head from pieces of pipe and other materials that fly through the air when they are using cutting tools.

Footwear

Plumbers have footwear with steel toes and soles that are made so that they do not slip on wet floors. Plumbers also work in areas with electrical lines and switches. Plumbers need footwear that has **insulated** soles that protect them from electric shocks.

Gloves

Plumbers protect their hands from sharp objects and tools. Their hands also come into contact with different chemicals and materials. Plumbers often wear rubber gloves. This gives them extra protection from the **germs** in drains. Plumbers wear thick gloves when working with hot pipes so they do not get burned.

Tools of the Trade

Plumbers use many different types of tools in their work. They use wrenches, vises, pliers, and tools for cutting and joining pipe. Pliers are used to grip pipe when needed. Vises are used to hold pipe in place while it is being cut. This makes sure that the cut is straight. Plumbers use these types of tools for plumbing problems such as blockages. Sometimes, video cameras are used to find problems in pipes or hidden leaks.

Pliers
Plumbers use pliers to grip and turn pipe fittings, nuts, and bolts. The teeth on the jaws grip the object firmly. The size of the jaws can be adjusted. Plumbers' pliers are made of steel. They have long handles covered with plastic.

Wrenches
Wrenches hold pipe and turn plumbing parts when fitting them. They also tighten nuts and bolts. Wrenches come in different sizes. Some are used with brass or polished pipe so that the metal will not be damaged.

Cutting Tools
Hacksaws have different blades for different jobs. They are used to cut pieces of metal pipe. Pipe cutters are mainly used to cut plastic pipe. They make cleaner and more level cuts. After pipes are cut, plumbers smooth the edges with files and pipe cleaning brushes.

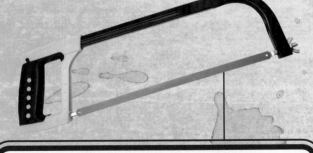

Plungers

A plunger is a tool that can be used to unblock drains. It has a rubber cone fixed to a handle. The plunger is pushed down over a plug hole and then released to suck out any material that might be causing the blockage.

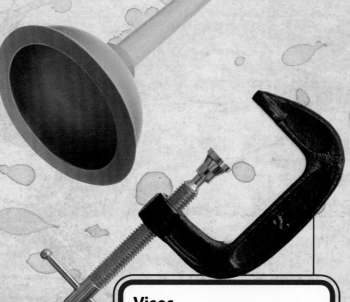

Vises

Vises hold pipes in place while the pipes are cut. They can also be used when pieces of pipe are joined together. Some vises use chain to hold the pipe in place. The vises can be mounted on a **tripod**. They can then be moved around the job site.

Then

The first plumbing systems in North America used wooden pipes. These were made from hollow logs. Wooden pipes sometimes cracked or broke underground. After 1800, cast iron pipes began to be used. These pipes were stronger and lasted longer.

Now

Today, plumbers use different materials for pipes. Copper is mostly used for water pipes. Steel is used for pipes that carry gas. Pipes are also made out of plastic. These cost less than other pipes. They are also less likely be become blocked.

The Plumber's Role

Many buildings have water for drinking or **sanitation**. Many also use gas for cooking or heating. Plumbers are an important part of the construction team that builds new buildings. Older buildings also need equipment to be repaired or replaced.

Most people have to call a plumber at some point. Sometimes, there are not enough plumbers to do all the jobs. This means that there is always work. People also need plumbers to fix things right away, at any time of day or night. This means that plumbers can sometimes be paid very well. People are very grateful for the work that plumbers do to fix problems. No one wants to live for too long without water to drink or wash with.

Plumbing is part of every day life, especially in homes. Flushing uses 25 percent of a home's water. Washing clothes uses 20 percent. Watering lawns and gardens uses 10 percent of the water supply.

Wrenches are used to tighten the pipes that drain water from kitchen sinks.

Saving Water

There is not enough water in some parts of the country. Water is needed for farms as well as for houses. Today, it is very important to not waste water. There are many ways to make plumbing more efficient and less harmful to the environment.

Low-flush toilets use **2 to 5** times less water than normal toilets.

Energy-efficient dishwashers and clothes washers can **reduce** the appliances' water use by up to **50 percent.**

Collected rainwater can be used for non-drinking purposes.

Becoming a Plumber

To become a plumber, people have to have the right skills and attitude. This job requires lifting heavy objects. Plumbers also deal with dirt and smells. They work outside the normal workday and can be called to emergencies in the middle of the night. Plumbers need to be in good physical shape to do their work. They need a high school diploma. Plumbers also have on the job training and study in classrooms.

Salaries in the plumbing industry vary in different areas of the United States. Plumbers are paid more money if they have more experience and knowledge of the job. Some plumbers are also experts in certain types of piping systems.

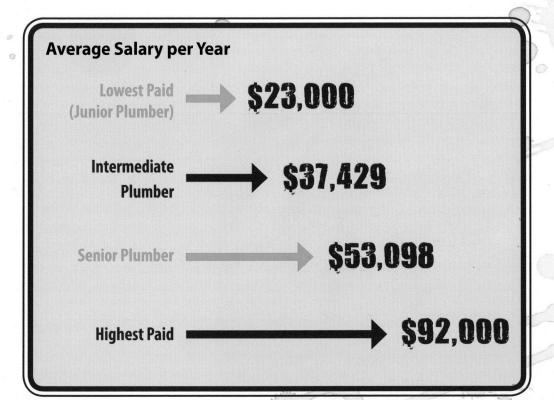

Average Salary per Year

Lowest Paid (Junior Plumber) → **$23,000**

Intermediate Plumber → **$37,429**

Senior Plumber → **$53,098**

Highest Paid → **$92,000**

Although more women are choosing plumbing as a career, they only make up about 10 percent of all plumbers.

Is This Career For You?

Careers in plumbing are not for everyone. You may have some or all of the skills required. However, you may not always be installing new equipment. You might be uncomfortable working with sewers or blocked drains. If you feel this way, you may need to think about a different career. It is also important to remember that some plumbers are **self-employed**.

☑ **Training**

Plumbers complete on-the-job training with experienced colleagues. This is called an apprenticeship where they learn all about the job. This takes about four or five years. They also take some classroom courses during their training.

☑ **Education**

Get a high school diploma, and take some math courses. You will need math skills to take measurements and work out plumbing specifications. After training as an apprentice, you take an exam. In some areas, you may need to be licensed and certified. This means that you can apply for better plumbing jobs.

☑ **Application**

Contact local plumbing, heating, and air conditioning companies about available positions. City government might also have openings. Some positions are advertised on the internet or on job boards.

Career Connections

Plan your plumbing career with this activity. Follow the instructions in the steps below to complete the process of becoming a plumber.

 1. Speak to your local plumbers. They can answer your questions and give you an inside look into the position.

 2. Visit a job fair or a college career center to find out more information about working as a plumber.

3. Work on your resumé. A good resumé that shows your strongest skills can go a long way toward attracting the attention of potential employers.

 **4.** Call or write to a plumbing company. Say that you are interested in a plumber position and ask for advice on how to apply.

1. Decide if you have the personality and attitude for being a plumber. If you do not mind a dirty job, can work long hours including evenings, weekends, and holidays, and are in good physical shape, this may be the job for you.

2. Think about the skills you will need to have.

3. Contact employers for requirements. Look for private and public plumbing companies. Get in touch with them, and find out what they are looking for from potential applicants.

4. Apply for the position, and arrange an interview. If successful, come to the interview with knowledge of the industry and your skills.

Quiz

1. Low-flow showers and faucets can reduce home water use by how much?

2. How many hours do plumbers typically work each day?

3. What does a plunger do?

4. What is the average salary for a junior plumber?

5. What percentage of plumbers are self-employed?

6. What is the poisonous gas that forms in sewers?

7. What are vises used for?

8. Why is mold in warm, damp areas a danger to plumbers?

9. How many plumbers, pipefitters, and steamfitters were working in the U.S. in 2012?

10. What percentage of plumbers are women?

Answers:
1. Up to 60 percent 2. 8 to 10 hours 3. It helps unblock pipes using suction. 4. $23,000 5. About 11 percent. 6. Hydrogen sulphide 7. To hold pipes in place while they are being cut 8. Exposure to mold can cause breathing problems 9. 386, 900 10. About 10 percent

Key Words

asbestos: a fire resistant material used in construction; inhaling its dust is a health hazard

biohazards: biological or chemical substances that are dangerous to humans

cast iron: a very hard metal that is made into different shapes

drainage: systems that empty liquid from areas such as kitchens and bathrooms

faucets: devices that control the flow of water from a pipe

germs: a substance that causes disease

insulated: covered with a substance that stops heat or electricity from getting in

irrigation: watering land by artificial means

Latin: the language of Ancient Rome

sanding: polishing or smoothing with sandpaper

sanitation: the disposal of sewage and solid waste

self-employed: working for oneself rather than for an employer

sewage: liquid and solid waste that is carried in drains

sulfur dioxide: a strong smelling gas that is poisonous

tradespeople: people who have professions with special skills that are usually done with the hands, such as plumbers, builders, and electricians

tripod: a stand that has three legs and is used for mounting equipment such as cameras and vises

Index

Log on to www.av2books.com

AV² by Weigl brings you media enhanced books that support active learning. Go to www.av2books.com, and enter the special code found on page 2 of this book. You will gain access to enriched and enhanced content that supplements and complements this book. Content includes video, audio, weblinks, quizzes, a slide show, and activities.

AV² Online Navigation

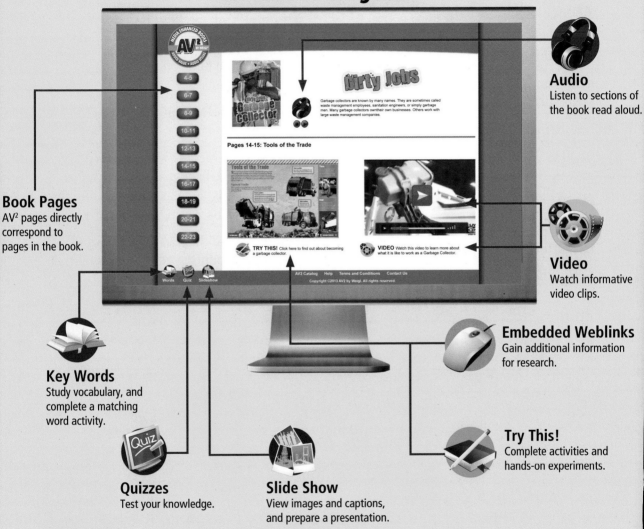

Book Pages
AV² pages directly correspond to pages in the book.

Audio
Listen to sections of the book read aloud.

Video
Watch informative video clips.

Key Words
Study vocabulary, and complete a matching word activity.

Quizzes
Test your knowledge.

Slide Show
View images and captions, and prepare a presentation.

Embedded Weblinks
Gain additional information for research.

Try This!
Complete activities and hands-on experiments.

AV² was built to bridge the gap between print and digital. We encourage you to tell us what you like and what you want to see in the future.

Sign up to be an AV² Ambassador at www.av2books.com/ambassador.

Due to the dynamic nature of the Internet, some of the URLs and activities provided as part of AV² by Weigl may have changed or ceased to exist. AV² by Weigl accepts no responsibility for any such changes. All media enhanced books are regularly monitored to update addresses and sites in a timely manner. Contact AV² by Weigl at 1-866-649-3445 or av2books@weigl.com with any questions, comments, or feedback.